Inspirational
Meditations

First published by Parragon in 2011

Parragon
Queen Street House
4 Queen Street
Bath BA1 1HE, UK

ISBN: 978-1-4454-3851-1

Printed in China

Inspirational
Meditations

a collection of inspirational thoughts and images

Bath • New York • Singapore • Hong Kong • Cologne • Delhi
Melbourne • Amsterdam • Johannesburg • Auckland • Shenzhen

All it takes is
one bloom
of hope
to make a
spiritual
garden.

Terri Guillemets

I will love the light for it shows me the way. Yet I will endure the darkness for it shows me the stars.

Og Mandino

It is not because things are difficult that we do not dare, it is because we do not dare that they are difficult.

Seneca

Beauty and grace
command the world.

Park Benjamin

Simplicity is making the journey of this life with just baggage enough.

Anonymous

A **hero** is a man who is **afraid** to run away.

Proverb

If I have **seen** further, it is by standing on the shoulders of giants.

Isaac Newton

Our sorrows and wounds are healed only when we touch them with compassion.

Buddha

19

Gratitude

is not only the greatest of virtues, but the parent of all the others.

Cicero

No trumpets SOUND when the important

decisions of our life are made.
Destiny is made known silently.

Agnes de Mille

The great thing in this world is not so much where we are, but in what direction we are moving.

Oliver Wendell Holmes

If you have
knowledge,
let others light
their candles in it.

Margaret Fuller

The real voyage of discovery consists not in seeking new landscapes, but in having new eyes.

Marcel Proust

Nothing is predestined:
The obstacles of your past
can become the gateways
that lead to new beginnings.

Ralph Blum

This **above** all:
to thine own self be **true.**

William Shakespeare

We must become
the change
we want to see.

Mahatma Gandhi

The best way to
prepare for life
is to begin to live.

Elbert Hubbard

If you could get
up the courage
to begin, you have the
courage to succeed.

David Viscott

True strength lies in submission which permits one to dedicate his life, through devotion, to something beyond himself.

Arthur Miller

Better a diamond with a flaw than a pebble without.

Confucius

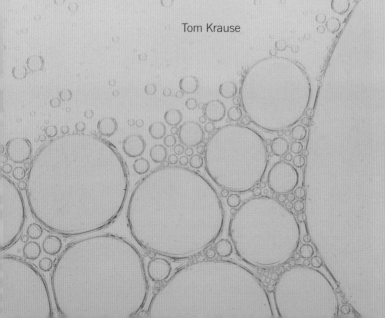

Courage is the discovery
that you may not win,
and trying when you
know you can lose.

Tom Krause

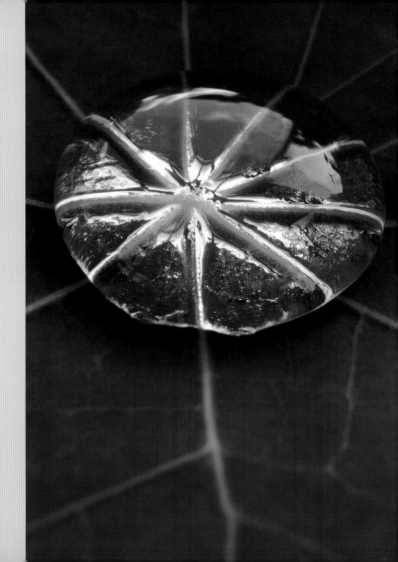

All misfortune

is but a stepping stone

to fortune.

Henry David Thoreau

Concentration
is the secret of
strength.

Ralph Waldo Emerson

Take rest; a field that has rested gives a bountiful crop.

Ovid

Confidence
is half of victory.

Yiddish Proverb

Success is the
good fortune that
comes from aspiration,
desperation, perspiration
and inspiration.

Evan Esar

Better to light a candle than to curse the darkness.

Chinese Proverb

Knowing

yourself is the

beginning of all

wisdom.

Aristotle

Life isn't about
finding yourself.
Life is about
creating yourself.

George Bernard Shaw

Don't let what you can't do stop you from doing what you can do.

John Wooden

The best
motivation
always comes
from within.

Michael Johnson

The only journey
is the journey within.

Rainer Maria Rilke

I want to be all
that I am capable of
becoming.

Katherine Mansfield

The true meaning of life is to plant trees, under whose shade you do not expect to sit.

Nelson Henderson

The words of kindness
are more healing
to a drooping heart
than balm or honey.

Sarah Fielding

Collect as precious pearls
the words of the wise
and virtuous.

Abd-el-Kadar

He that will not reflect is a ruined man.

Asian Proverb

Happiness

is not a station

you arrive at,

but a manner

of traveling.

Margaret Runbeck

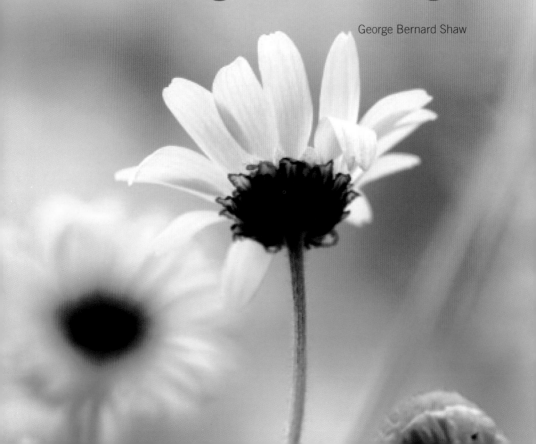

Life is not meant to be easy, my child; but take courage – it can be delightful.

George Bernard Shaw

Patience, persistence and perspiration make an unbeatable combination for success.

Napoleon Hill

The world breaks everyone, and afterward many are strong in the broken places.

Ernest Hemingway

No law or ordinance
is mightier than
understanding.

Plato

Really great
people make you feel
that you, too, can
become great.

Mark Twain

The highest reward
for a person's toil is not
what they get for it, but what
they become by it.

John Ruskin

When I let go
of what I am,
I become what
I might be.

Lao Tzu

Everything is okay in the end, if it's not ok, then it's not the end.

Anonymous

Picture credits